WHAT·DO·WE·KNOW
ABOUT 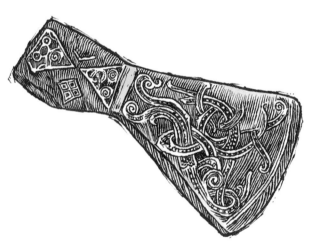 THE
VIKINGS·?

HAZEL MARY MARTELL

PETER BEDRICK BOOKS

NEW YORK

First American edition published in 1992 by
Peter Bedrick Books
2112 Broadway
New York, NY 10023

Published by agreement with
Simon & Schuster Young Books,
Hemel Hempstead, England

Library of Congress Cataloging-in-Publication Data
Martell, Hazel.
    What do we know about the Vikings?/Hazel Mary Martell. – 1st American ed.
    Includes index.
    Summary: Provides information about the history, daily life, social structure, and culture of
    the Vikings.
    ISBN 0–87226–355–X
    1. Vikings – Social life and customs – Juvenile literature.
    2. Northmen – Social life and customs – Juvenile literature.
    [1. Vikings.]   I. Title
    DL31.M29   1992
940.1′4 – dc20   92–7893
                                                                          CIP
                                                                          AC

Design: David West
           Children's Book Design

Illustrator: Rob Shone

Copy editor: Ros Mair

Photograph acknowledgements:
Cover front: WF/Statens Historiska Museum, Stockholm; Aalborg Historiske Museum:
p13(t); Courtesy, Canadian Parks Service: p38; Martyn F. Chillmaid: p14, p15(b), p16; C.M.
Dixon: p17(r), p20, p26(b), p28, p31, p40; Forhistorisk Museum, Moesgard: p19; Werner
Forman Archive: p7, p9, p17(1), p30, WF/National Museum, Copenhagen: p33(t), p34(b),
WF/Statens Historiska Museum, Stockholm: p26(t), p32, WF/Stofnun Arnamagnussonar,
Iceland: p33(b), WF/Viking Ships Museum, Bygdy, Oslo: p36–37; Robert Harding Picture
Library: p8(t), p14, p29(1); Michael Holford: endpapers, p12–13, p22(b), p25(b), p29(r),
p37(b), p39(b), p40(1), p41, p42; National Museum of Ireland, Dublin: p22(t); Skyggna
Myndverk: p18(b); Statens Historiska Museum: p15(t); Stofnun Arnamagnussonar, Iceland:
p12(t), p31(t); Universitetets Oldsaksamling, Oslo: p34–5, p37(t); David Williams: p18(t),
p39(t); York Archaeological Trust Picture Library, p8(b), p21, p23, p24, p25(t), p35(b),
p40(r).

Picture research: Jennie Karrach

Typeset by: Goodfellow and Egan, Cambridge

Printed and bound by: BPCC Hazell Books, Paulton
and Aylesbury, England.

Endpapers: This Viking carving was excavated from St Paul's Churchyard, London. It shows a
battle between a lion and a serpent and dates from around AD 1030. It stands 18 inches high
and was set up by two Vikings called Ginna and Toki.

· CONTENTS ·

WHO·WERE · THE · VIKINGS?

Look at the two maps on the opposite page. The small one shows the countries the Vikings came from. The large one shows the places they went to between AD 780 and 1100. This period is known as the Viking Age. Not long ago, people thought it was a time of terror and destruction. They only knew about the Viking raids on monasteries and towns. But the Vikings were also great adventurers. They set up trading links and they looked for new lands where they could settle down and farm. They were also fierce fighters and won most of their early battles. They never had an empire, but from 1030 to 1035 the King of Denmark also ruled England and Norway.

THE VIKING HOMELANDS

The Vikings had many reasons for leaving their homelands at the end of the eighth century. One reason was that the population had started to increase. This meant that more people wanted land of their own. However, there was not enough good land for them all in Scandinavia. As this photograph shows, Norway is very mountainous with only a small amount of farmland. And a lot of Sweden is covered in forests and marshes.

METAL WORKERS

Iron ore was plentiful throughout the Viking lands. It was often found near the surface in marshy ground and so did not have to be mined. The Vikings smelted small amounts of this ore to make metal. They then made the metal into tools and household equipment, such as axes, hammerheads, nails and pans. Skilled workers made swords like the one below.

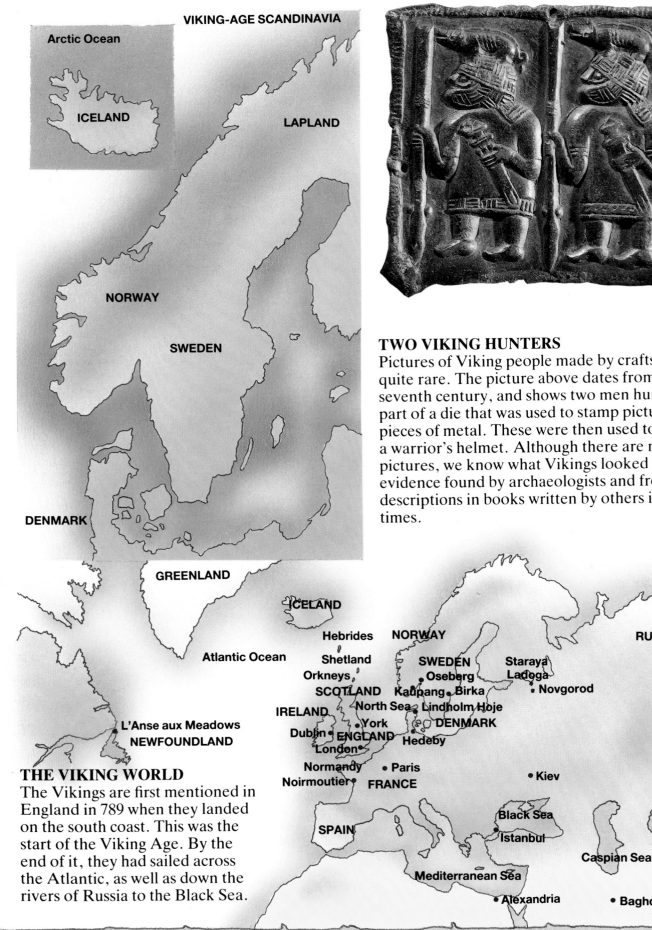

VIKING-AGE SCANDINAVIA

Arctic Ocean

ICELAND

LAPLAND

NORWAY

SWEDEN

DENMARK

TWO VIKING HUNTERS

Pictures of Viking people made by craftsmen are quite rare. The picture above dates from the seventh century, and shows two men hunting. It is part of a die that was used to stamp pictures onto pieces of metal. These were then used to decorate a warrior's helmet. Although there are not many pictures, we know what Vikings looked like from evidence found by archaeologists and from descriptions in books written by others in Viking times.

GREENLAND

ICELAND

Hebrides

NORWAY

RUSSIA

Atlantic Ocean

Shetland

SWEDEN

Staraya
Ladoga

Orkneys

Oseberg

Bolgar

SCOTLAND

Kaupang Birka

Novgorod

North Sea Lindholm Hoje

IRELAND

York

DENMARK

Dublin ENGLAND Hedeby

L'Anse aux Meadows
NEWFOUNDLAND

London

Normandy Paris

Kiev

Noirmoutier FRANCE

THE VIKING WORLD

The Vikings are first mentioned in England in 789 when they landed on the south coast. This was the start of the Viking Age. By the end of it, they had sailed across the Atlantic, as well as down the rivers of Russia to the Black Sea.

SPAIN

Black Sea

Istanbul

Caspian Sea

Mediterranean Sea

Alexandria

Baghdad

	750—800	850	875	900	925
THE VIKINGS AT HOME	Population growth in Norway, Sweden and Denmark leads to farmers looking for new land. The Oseberg ship is built around 800.	Vikings continue to leave their homelands and settle overseas as farmers and traders. The Oseberg ship was probably buried around 850. The Gokstad ship was built around 850.	The Gokstad ship is buried between 860 and 900. More Danish Vikings leave home to settle in England.	Harald Finehair becomes the first King of all Norway. Vikings who object to this go to live abroad.	Many Vikings from Norway go to live in Iceland. They take their families and belongings, including their animals, in open-decked ships.
IN NORTHERN EUROPE	The first Viking raids are in England in 789 and 793. Later they attack the Scottish islands and the coast of Ireland.	Vikings settle in the Orkneys and Shetlands. Raids on England start in 835. In 850 the Vikings stay in England for their first winter. The Great Army from Denmark arrives in England in 866 and captures York in 867.	In England the Vikings are defeated at the battle of Edington in 878 by Alfred the Great. In 886 he draws up a treaty allowing them to settle in the Danelaw. In 885 Paris is besieged again.	The King of France gives Normandy to the Viking leader Rollo in 911. In exchange he and his men help defend France from other Viking attacks.	The Vikings in Normandy settle down and become Christians. Many marry local women. Eventually they will forget their Viking ways.
BEYOND NORTHERN EUROPE		Vikings reach Spain in 844, but are defeated by the Arabs. Swedish Vikings visit Russia. By 860 they reach and attack Constantinople (now Istanbul). Other Vikings sail into the Mediterranean.	Iceland is discovered and settlement starts in 874. Swedish Vikings set up trading towns at Novgorod, Smolensk and Kiev in Russia. Then they visit Constantinople and Baghdad and bring back goods from as far away as China.	Greenland is probably first sighted by a Viking blown off-course on his way from Norway to Iceland. An Arab, Ibn Fadlan, writes a detailed account of a Viking cremation in Russia in 922.	By 930 there are around 10,000 Vikings living in Iceland.
EVENTS AROUND THE WORLD	Paper-making spreads from China to the Muslim world, which includes North Africa, Spain and Arabia.	The first book ever printed appears in China in 861. Alfred the Great becomes King of Wessex, England, in 871. Polynesian colonists start to settle in New Zealand. They are the ancestors of the Maoris.		Arab merchants settle on the East African coast at Manda and Kilwa. In China the Tang dynasty ends in 907.	

Scythe

Viking ship

Sword

Merchant's scales

| --- | --- | --- | --- | --- |
In Denmark fortresses such as Trelleborg and Fyrkat are built.	Hakon the Good, the first Christian king of Norway, dies in 960. In the same year King Harald Bluetooth of Denmark is baptized. Olaf Tryggvason becomes King of Norway in 995.	Christianity spreads through their homelands. The Swedish Vikings keep their old gods the longest. Svein Forkbeard is King of Denmark.	King Olaf Haraldsson of Norway is killed in battle in 1030. He later becomes a saint. Harald Hardradi becomes King of Norway in 1047. Two years later he burns down the Danish market town of Hedeby.	Harald Hardradi of Norway claims the throne of England, but is killed at the battle of Stamford Bridge in 1066.
Thor's hammer  The last Viking king of York, Eirik Bloodaxe, is killed at the battle of Stainmore in 954.	In 980 the Irish defeat the Vikings at the battle of Tara. There are fresh Viking attacks on England. The English are defeated by the Vikings at the battle of Malden in 991 and from then on a great amount of Danegeld is paid out.	In 1014 Brian Boru, king of the Irish, defeats the Vikings at the battle of Clontarf. In 1016 the Danish Vikings defeat the English at the battle of Ashingdon. Svein Forkbeard becomes king of England and is followed by his son, Canute.	After the death of Olaf Haraldsson, Canute becomes King of Norway and King of Denmark and England. In 1035 Canute is followed by his son, Harthacanute. He dies suddenly in 1042 and Edward the Confessor is chosen as King of England.	
In Constantinople the Emperor's private army, called the Varangian Guard, is made up mainly of Vikings.	Eirik the Red discovers Greenland in 980. Five years later Vikings from Iceland start to settle there. In 986 Bjarni Herjolfsson sees the coast of North America, but does not go ashore.	The people of Iceland decide to become Christian in 1000. Leif Eirikson sails from Greenland and reaches Newfoundland, which he calls Vinland. Thorfinn Karselfni tries to settle in Vinland, but leaves after three years.	The great Viking explorations come to an end.	By 1100 the Viking Age is over. **Helmet**
Viking warrior The Toltecs rise to power in Central Mexico. England is reunited under one king after the death of Eirik Bloodaxe.	Ethelred the Unready becomes King of England in 978. The Vikings take advantage of this weak ruler.	In 1002 Ethelred orders the killing of all Danish Vikings in southern England. This event leads Svein Forkbeard to attack England.		In America the Anasazi start building Cliff Palace at Mesa Verde in Colorado.

THE AGE OF MIGRATIONS

The Viking Age came near the end of a longer period of time which is called the Age of Migrations in Europe. This started around the beginning of the fifth century AD when many people were on the move across the continent. Some used their skills as sailors to cross the North Sea and attack Britain. At first they were looking for places to rob and plunder for gold and other treasure. Later they started looking for other places where they could settle down and farm. At the same time, the Roman Empire was collapsing. Roman soldiers were leaving Britain, France and Germany to defend themselves. The people who were on the move took advantage of this. Those known as Angles, Jutes, Frisians and Saxons moved to England and set up new kingdoms there. By the end of the eighth century, it was the turn of these kingdoms to be attacked, as the Vikings left their homelands to look for plunder, land and trade.

THE LAST VIKING KINGS

In 1066 Harald Hardradi of Norway claimed the throne of England, but he was then killed at the Battle of Stamford Bridge. King Harold of England took the throne, but he was then defeated by the Normans.

DID·THE ·VIKINGS· GROW·THEIR OWN·FOOD?

Most of the Vikings were farmers who grew their own food. They usually had fairly small farms and just grew enough to feed their own families. In their fields they grew grain crops such as oats, barley, wheat and rye. They also grew vegetables such as cabbages, onions and beans around the house. They kept geese and goats, as well as sheep, cattle, pigs and hens. Some of the sheep, cattle and pigs were killed at the end of summer and their meat preserved for the winter. The rest were fed on the hay which had been dried over the summer.

FISHING
Nearly all Viking farms were near the sea. Because of this, most Vikings went fishing. The ones in the picture above have caught a whale, but usually they caught fish such as cod or herring. They used a net or a hook on a line and some even managed to spear fish from a boat. When the fish had been caught, some were eaten right away. Others were preserved.

FARMING
The picture below is from the Bayeux Tapestry. The tapestry was made at the end of the Viking Age, but farming methods had not changed much throughout the period. First the land was plowed, then the seeds were scattered on it by hand. A horse-drawn harrow then covered the seeds with soil. After this, the children helped to chase the birds off until the seeds started to grow.

A PLOWED FIELD

A lot of the land that the Vikings farmed is still farmed today. This means that most of the evidence for Viking farming has disappeared. However, some farms were abandoned after the Viking Age and grass grew over the plowed fields. In the center of this picture you can see the remains of an old plowed field in a place where the soil has not been disturbed since Viking times.

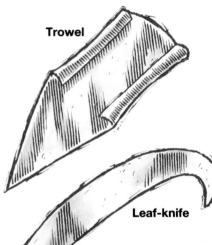
Quern

MAKING FLOUR

The Vikings made flour with a quern, like the one reconstructed on the right. It was made of two hard stones. Grain was dropped through a hole in the top stone. This was then turned round and round over the bottom stone until the grain had been ground into flour.

FARM TOOLS

The Vikings had no powered machinery such as tractors to help them on their farms. They had horses to pull the plows and the harrows, but the other work was done by hand. They had long-handled scythes to cut the hay, sickles to cut the grain crops, hoes for weeding and spades for digging. Picks were useful for breaking up stones, axes for felling trees.

Trowel

Leaf-knife

Scythe

 THE VIKING SUMMER

Spring was a busy time on the farm with fields to plow and seeds to sow. The hayfields also had to be spread with manure to make the grass grow. When he had finished this work, the farmer probably went raiding or trading for the summer. His wife and children would then look after the farm. In Norway they took the cattle and sheep to mountain pastures for the summer. Then the grass around the farm was cut for hay. At the end of summer the farmer came back in time for the harvest, and the animals were brought back to the farm.

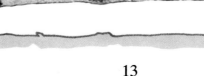

DID·THE VIKINGS ·GO· SHOPPING?

Most Vikings lived in small settlements with no shops, so they made most of the things they needed. This included clothes, as well as tools and furniture. However, some towns did become trading centers. The main ones were Hedeby in Denmark, Birka in Sweden, Kaupang in Norway and Jorvik (York) in England. In these towns the Vikings could buy luxury goods, such as silk, brocade, glassware and wine. Craftsmen such as jewelers and shoemakers also worked in the towns. They sold their goods at their workshops. Some used salesmen.

POTS AND WOODWARE

This photograph shows some reconstructions of Viking-Age pottery and woodware. They are based on archaeological discoveries made in York, which the Vikings called Jorvik. The street in which they were found is called Coppergate. This name probably comes from two Viking words – *koppr*, meaning cup, and *gat*, street.

Viking cups and plates were rarely made of clay, however. Most were made from wood. All towns had woodworkers, but potters were more unusual. Wood soon rots in the ground, but enough pieces were found in York for the archaeologists to reconstruct some of them in new wood. Although clay pots were fragile, they were often transported over long distances. Pottery from Germany has been found throughout the Viking lands.

HACK SILVER

The early Vikings traded their goods for other things of equal value, or exchanged them for silver jewelery. Finger-rings and arm-rings were worn by both men and women. When they needed money, they hacked pieces of silver off these rings. This was weighed on scales and used as money.

THE SHOPS AT JORVIK

This picture shows a Viking workshop which has been rebuilt at the Jorvik museum in York. The shopfront was open to the street, and all the goods were displayed on a wooden shelf. This shop belonged to a leather worker. As well as making shoes, he made straps and belts and harnesses for horses. Other goods on sale in Jorvik included wooden spoons, glass and amber beads, silver jewelery, combs and wine.

Wooden spoon

MAKING A COIN

Viking-Age coins were hand-made by a man called a "moneyer". He engraved one side of the coin in reverse on a metal die (1) and tested it on a strip of lead to make sure it was correct. He then placed the die on a strip of silver (2) and tapped it sharply with a hammer to make an imprint. When he had made a series of imprints of one side (3), he separated them (4). Then he turned them over and stamped the other side with a different die.

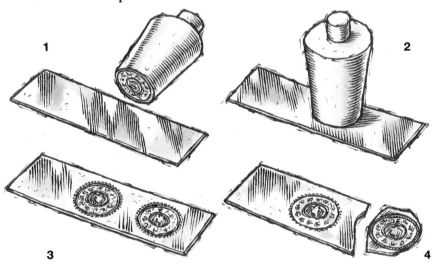

EVIDENCE

Much of what we know about the goods sold in Viking shops comes from evidence dug up by archaeologists. In York they could only excavate, or dig up, a small area as the site of Jorvik has been built over many times since the Viking Age. But in Denmark and Sweden the old market towns of Hedeby and Birka had been abandoned. Hedeby was never rebuilt after being attacked and set on fire in 1069. Birka lost its trade – the sea level dropped and ships could no longer get there. At both these sites the archaeologists found remains of luxury goods, such as glassware and silks. There were also everyday items, such as pins, needles and spoons.

DID · THE VIKINGS · HAVE · FAMILIES LIKE · OURS?

A Viking's idea of a family was a bit different from ours. It included not only parents and children, but also cousins, aunts and uncles. Often grandparents, parents and children lived together in the same house. The Vikings took kinship very seriously. They thought that loyalty to the family was more important than loyalty to a leader or ruler. Sometimes this loyalty led to problems. For example, if someone was murdered, his family would go and murder someone from the killer's family. This could start a long-lasting feud between the families. Some feuds lasted for two or three generations and involved distant relations such as second or third cousins.

THE FAMILY AT HOME

The most important place in the Viking home was the fireplace or hearth. The fire was important both for heat and light, and food was cooked over it. The family would gather round it, just as the actors are doing in the reconstructions above.

Despite this closeness, many Viking boys were sent to a foster family at the age of ten. Sometimes this family was related to the boy. More often the foster father and the boy's own father were foster brothers themselves. Their ties were almost as strong as family ties.

VIKING WOMEN

The Swedish pendant on the left shows a Viking woman. In real life she was treated with respect. She was allowed to choose her own husband or stay single if she wanted to. She could also own property whether she was single or married. When her husband was away, she was in charge of the house and could do business on his behalf.

A MEMORIAL STONE

Not all Vikings who went raiding and trading returned home safely. Some were killed in fights or accidents. Others died of diseases. When this happened, the families put up a carved stone in their memory. This one is at Broby in Sweden. The writing around the outside is in runes. It tells us that the stone was put up by a woman called Estrid. It is in memory of her husband who had visited Jerusalem and died in Greece.

MARRIAGE

Viking men and women could choose their own partners. They did not need their parents' consent to get married. If one set of parents did not approve, however, this sometimes led to a feud between the two families. Most marriages took place in the early winter when everyone was at home. The event was celebrated with a great feast, involving friends and neighbors, as well as relations. It could last as long as two weeks. As well as eating and drinking, there was entertainment, which included poetry, music and dancing. If the marriage did not work, the Vikings could get divorced. This was a very simple matter. All the husband or wife had to do was made a formal speech in front of witnesses, saying why they did not want to be married any longer.

USEFUL TOOLS

Viking clothes did not have pockets and Viking women did not have handbags. Instead, they carried the things they needed on a long chain, suspended from a brooch. These things included sewing needles made out of fine bones, which were kept in a case made from a larger, hollow bone. A woman also carried keys to any storage chests in the house, a knife, small shears or scissors, a small whetstone to sharpen the blades and a comb.

Needles

Keys

Knife

Knife sheath

DID · THE VIKINGS LIVE · IN HOUSES ?

Most Viking families lived on farms in the country. Their houses were known as longhouses because of their shape. Often they only had one large room, or hall, in which everybody ate, slept and did the household chores. Sometimes the barn for the animals was built on to the end of the house and was connected to it by a door. Only a small number of Vikings lived in towns. When they did, their houses were often built to the same pattern as the farmhouses. They were at a right angle to the street and often had a workshop or a warehouse attached to them.

THE FARMHOUSE AT STONG
There are few Viking houses left today. One reason is that the Vikings usually built in wood which has long since rotted away. Another reason is that many Viking farms were on land which is still farmed today. However, the farm at Stong in Iceland was abandoned around 1104 when a volcano erupted, covering the land with ash. The house was excavated by archaeologists in 1939. They found enough evidence to make the reconstruction shown below. The walls were made of blocks of turf, as shown on the left. The roof was made of turf that kept on growing. The farmhouse had a living room, a hall, a dairy and a lavatory.

FURNITURE

The Vikings did not have much furniture. Only the farmer and his wife would sleep in a bed. Everyone else got wrapped up in blankets and animal skins and slept on a raised platform along the wall of the room. Spare clothes and other belongings were kept in chests.

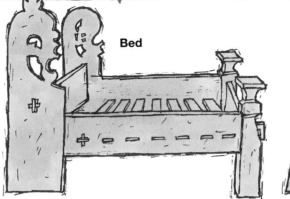

Bed

Chest

KITCHEN UTENSILS

The kitchen was quite well-equipped. As dairy foods made up a large part of the diet, there were butter churns and cheese drainers. They stored food in wooden tubs and barrels, including flour. However, it seems that most kitchens did not have fine sieves. Flour often contained bits of stone off the quern, which wore the Vikings' teeth down!

Wooden tub

Knife

Wooden bowls

Cheese drainer

INSIDE A HOUSE

This is the inside of a Viking house that has been reconstructed in Denmark. The hearth is in the middle of the floor, which is made of beaten earth. A large cooking pot is suspended from a chain from the roof. To the left of the door there is a loom for weaving. Opposite is the bed. When the fire was burning, the room filled with smoke as there was no chimney.

EATING MEALS

Vikings usually ate two meals each day. Their first was eaten around eight o'clock in the morning and the second around seven o'clock at night. They ate off trestle tables which were set up specially. The master of the house and his wife sat in a chair called the "high seat". Everyone else sat on the edge of the platforms built out from the walls. Sometimes there were linen cloths on the tables. Food was eaten from wooden bowls or plates. There were spoons and knives, but no forks.

WHO · WENT TO · WORK · IN THE · VIKING · L A N D S ? ·

Most Vikings were freemen, known as *karls*. Most of them owned their own land and worked for themselves. Their wives and children helped with a lot of the work. A *karl* who had no land could work for another *karl*. There were also slaves, or *thralls*, who did the heavy and dirty work like spreading manure and digging up iron ore. Some Vikings were traders as well as farmers, some were craftsmen. They made things like combs from deer antlers, jewelery, shoes, and weapons, which the farmers might not be able to make for themselves.

MAKING A SWORD

This woodcarving shows a scene from the legend of Sigurd the Dragon-slayer. He and another Viking warrior are making a sword. Sigurd is working the bellows to keep the fire hot, while Reginn is hammering the blade of the sword.

Swords were made from several rods of iron, twisted together while they were hot. They were then hammered flat to make a smooth blade. The blade was edged with steel and sharpened. The twisted rods in the middle made the sword more flexible, and gave it a pattern like snake skin. Some swords had names such as Adder and Leg-biter.

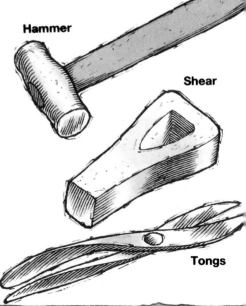

Hammer

Shear

Tongs

BLACKSMITH'S TOOLS

A blacksmith in the Viking Age used tools that were very much like those used today. His hammer had an iron head, fixed on to a wooden handle. He smoothed rough edges off metal objects with a shear like the one on the right. His tongs, also made of iron, were used when he wanted to bend hot metal into shape. He also made more tools for himself and for other people. These included nails, axe-heads, shovels and plowshares.

MAKING BEADS

Craftsmen made beads from natural materials, such as jet, amber and crystal. They also made beads out of glass, like the ones shown here. They used recycled glass or imported it in small colored cubes, probably from northern Italy. The Vikings melted the glass in small crucibles, and pulled it into long sticks. The sticks were then wrapped round a metal rod. When they hardened, the rod was removed and the glass sliced into beads. Glass sticks of different colors could be twisted together to make patterned beads. Sometimes dots of colored glass in other colors were added.

Glass beads

MAKING A COMB

The Vikings made their combs from pieces of deer antler (1). They started by cutting a long strip (2), and splitting it into two identical pieces along its length. This was for the top. They cut several oblong pieces (3), to make the teeth. These were slotted between the two long pieces and fixed together with rivets. Then they were sawed into teeth (4). A pattern was often engraved along the top. Some combs had a hole drilled in one end so they could hang from a chain or a belt. Evidence of comb-making is found almost everywhere where the Vikings settled or traded.

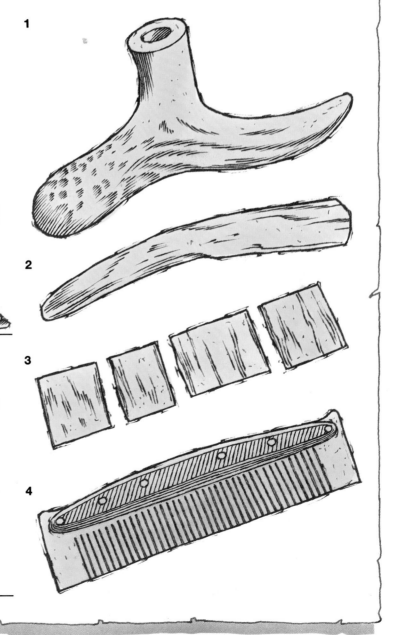

SLAVES

There were three groups of slaves in Viking society. The first group was made up of the children of slaves. The second group was prisoners taken in battle and the third group was people who had volunteered to become slaves. These were usually *karls* who had fallen on hard times. If they had no family to help them and no land on which they could grow food, *karls* could volunteer to become slaves. They had to give up all the rights they had as *karls*, but at least they were fed and had somewhere to live. Slaves had no rights and no property. However, a slave could work very hard and buy freedom for himself and his family.

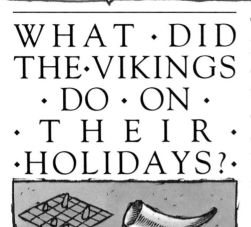

WHAT · DID THE · VIKINGS · DO · ON · THEIR · HOLIDAYS?

The Vikings did not go away on vacations, but they did have three religious celebrations each year. At the start of summer they celebrated Sigrblot. After the harvest, they celebrated Vetrarblot and just after midwinter they celebrated Jolablot. At all three there were feasts which could last two weeks. At others times the Vikings relaxed by playing games, including chess, ice-skating, wrestling, swimming, rowing in races and hunting.

GAMES AND SKILLS

Most Vikings were very competitive. In bad weather they challenged each other with board games, some played on boards like the one on the right. In good weather they liked outdoor sports, such as ball-games, including a sort of football. They held competitions to see who could swim furthest underwater, and had rowing races and wrestling matches. Another test was to see who could walk all the way around a longship by balancing on its oars as it was being rowed. These skills helped to keep them fit for real fighting.

CHESS

The three chessmen on the left are from a set found on the Isle of Lewis in the Hebrides. They were carved in the twelfth century. It is thought that Viking traders saw chess being played in Arabia and brought the game back home. It soon spread throughout the Viking lands. Other Viking board games included *hnefatafl*. This had one playing piece like a king, but the others were plain. No one is sure now how it was played, but probably the king had to be defended from the attackers on the other side.

ICE-SKATING

When the rivers froze, the Vikings got their skates out. These were made from the smoothed foot bones of cattle and horses. A hole was made in the front or back of the skate and a peg stuck in it. The skate was then tied to the shoe with a strip of leather. Skaters pushed themselves along the ice with poles.

GAMING PIECES

For their board games, the Vikings used playing-pieces made from wood, stone, ivory and glass. These drawings are based on pieces found in Birka. They might have come from as far away as Egypt.

DRINKING HORNS

Viking feasts involved a lot of drinking. They brewed beer and a drink called mead. They drank from horns, like the one below, which could not be put down. This meant that once the horn had been filled, the drinker had to drain it in one go.

Gambling pieces

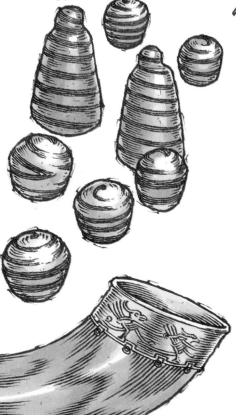

Drinking horn

SACRIFICES

The Viking word *blot* means sacrifice. At each of the three religious feasts, a horse was sacrificed to the gods. The Vikings were practical people, so this was often an old horse which could not work any more. If it was killed, its flesh was cooked and eaten by the Vikings at their feast. However, horses which were sacrificed were not always killed. The Vikings were prepared to strike a bargain with their gods. In this bargain they would agree to share the horse between them. It would stay with the Viking while it was alive and useful to him, but it would belong to the gods when it died. It is unlikely that the Vikings ever sacrificed people.

WHAT · DID THE VIKINGS · WEAR? ·

Archaeologists have found quite a lot of evidence for the clothes the Vikings wore. The rest comes from carvings in stone and wood and from written descriptions in Viking stories, their Sagas. From this, we know that the Vikings dressed for comfort, not fashion. The men wore tunics and tight-fitting trousers. Women wore an ankle-length dress made of linen, with a woollen tunic over the top. Everybody wore flat leather shoes, cloaks in cold weather and jewelery – but this was usually practical. Clothes were mainly home-made from fabric the women had woven themselves.

A VIKING FISHERMAN

This model of a Viking fisherman is in the Jorvik museum in York. His head and face were made by taking measurements from a real Viking skull and then reconstructing it.

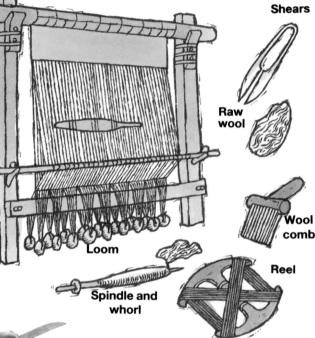

Shears

Raw wool

Wool comb

Reel

Loom

Spindle and whorl

MAKING CLOTH

Viking women made both woollen cloth and linen. Linen was made from the fibers of the flax plant. Sheep's wool was roughly cleaned, then combed to make all the hairs lie in the same direction. It was then spun into yarn with a spindle and whorl. This yarn was wound onto a reel and colored with vegetable dyes. It was then woven into cloth on an upright loom. Clay weights kept the warp (lengthwise) threads in place and a batten was used to straighten the weft (cross) threads as the cloth was woven.

SHOES

Viking shoes were made from leather. Sometimes farmers made them from the skins of cattle they killed on their farms. There were also shoemakers in the towns. To make a shoe, they needed a last, like the one on the right. It was made of wood and shaped like a foot. The shoe was formed around this. The sole and heel were made in one piece and the upper was sewn onto it. Most shoes were held on with a leather thong.

Tortoise brooches

HYGIENE

It is hard to decide whether the Vikings were clean or dirty. Men in England complained about the Vikings attracting the women because they combed their hair, bathed and changed their clothes so often! In contrast, Ibn Fadlan, an Arab who wrote about the Vikings, thought they were "the filthiest of God's creatures". He said they did not get washed often enough – and when they did, they all shared the same bowl of water. Another Arab who visited Hedeby around 950 wrote that both the men and the women wore eye make-up. From the number of combs found, it seems that the Vikings took care of their hair. Married women usually covered theirs with a scarf. Men fastened theirs back with a band, and kept their beards and moustaches neatly trimmed.

BROOCHES

The Vikings rarely used buttons and did not have zippers. Instead, they fastened their clothes with belts or brooches. The brooches shown above were called tortoise brooches because of their shape. They were hollow underneath and had a pin across the middle.

Viking women threaded this pin through a long loop attached to the back of their tunics and then through a shorter loop attached to the front. A string of beads showed how wealthy the family was. Other brooches were used to fasten shawls. Both men and women used large pins to fasten their cloaks in winter.

WHO · DID · THE · VIKINGS WORSHIP?

The early Vikings had no organized religion. They had no churches or temples and no priests or ceremonies. There were many different gods and goddesses, however, and most people believed in more than one. They thought the gods lived in a place called Asgard. The Vikings themselves lived in Midgard. Midgard was surrounded by a deep ocean and beyond this was Utgard where the Frost Giants lived. The Vikings believed that one day the Frost Giants would destroy all the gods in a final battle called Ragnarok and this would bring the world to an end.

Loki

STAVE CHURCHES

In the Vikings' homelands, there are still some ancient churches like this one at Borgund, on the Sognefjord in Norway. They are called stave churches because their walls are made of upright planks, or staves, of wood. By the time they were built, the Viking Age was over and the people of the Viking lands had become Christians. They still remembered the old gods, however, and put dragons as well as crosses on the church.

ODIN AND LOKI

Odin was the most important Viking god. He was wise and mysterious and was the god of poets, as well as the god of kings and warriors.
Odin's son Baldr was also a god. Legends said that Loki, the mischief-maker, was once punished on losing a wager by having his lips sewn together.

Odin

26

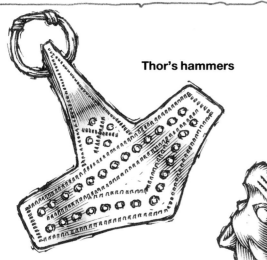

Thor's hammers

MAKING THOR'S HAMMER
The craftsman started by making a model of the hammer in wax (1). Then he made a mold by pressing the model between two pieces of soft clay (2). The mold was heated to melt the wax, which ran out of a hole in the mould, leaving an impression behind (3). Molten silver was poured into the mold. When the silver had hardened, the hammer was removed (4).

1

2

3

4

THOR AND HIS HAMMER
Thor was the most popular Viking god. He was thought to be a huge man with a red beard. He was fiery tempered, but also liked a good laugh. He made thunder rumble by riding across the sky in a chariot pulled by goats. Thor was not as clever as Odin and he had to use a hammer as a weapon in his battles with the giants. This hammer was called Mjollni and many Vikings had small copies of it made to wear as charms, or amulets. They thought these would protect them from misfortune and wicked creatures.

HOW THE VIKINGS BECAME CHRISTIANS

Vikings who traveled overseas were the first to become Christians. This was because it was easier to trade with Christian merchants if they all had the same religion. These Vikings were loyal to their old gods at home, however, and Christianity did not spread widely there until the late Viking Age.

The Vikings in Iceland took a vote on religion in the year 1000. Half the population wanted to become Christian and half wanted to stick with the old gods. The Lawspeaker finally chose Christianity and said that everyone should be baptized, but people could still worship the old gods in secret.

DID · THE VIKINGS BELIEVE · IN LIFE · AFTER · DEATH ? ·

Viking warriors thought that if they died on the battlefield, women called Valkyries would take them to a place called Valhalla. There they would be able to fight and "kill" each other all day long. In the evening they would go back to Odin's hall and be restored to life again. After eating and drinking the night away, they would be ready to go out and fight again. However, if they died in bed they would go to a cold, frosty place. Some Vikings were buried in their ships. Others had stones marking a boat-shape around their graves. Both men and women were given grave-goods for their journey to the next life.

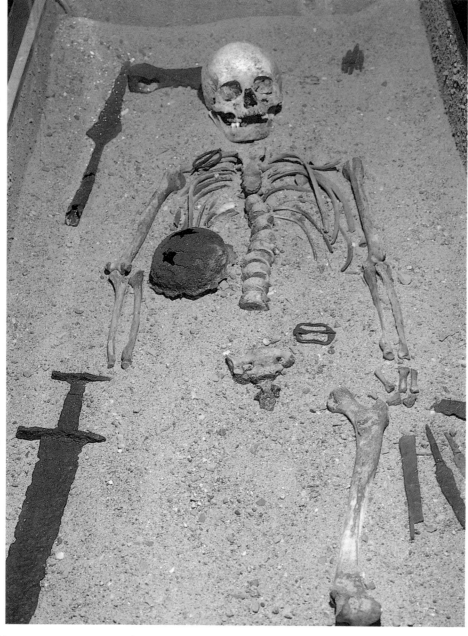

GRAVE-GOODS

This Viking warrior's grave was excavated in Norway. His sword was by his right hand and the remains of his shield were on his chest. There were several spear heads in his grave. Only part of his skeleton was left. As well as his weapons, a dead warrior was given food and drink for the journey to Valhalla. Traders were often buried with some of the goods they traded. At Oseberg in Norway a ship burial was excavated in 1904. It was the grave of a royal lady and contained many grave-goods, including a bed, four sledges, a wagon, and kitchen equipment. A servant was killed and buried with her to do all the work on the journey to the next life.

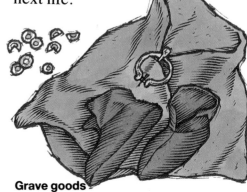

Grave goods

THE JOURNEY TO VALHALLA

On the right is a picture stone from Gotland in Sweden. The carvings show how Viking warriors who die in battle go straight to a kind of heaven known as Valhalla. This was considered the best way to die. The lower picture shows them traveling to Valhalla in a longship and the upper one shows one of them arriving there. He has been restored to life, given a horse and is being welcomed by one of Odin's Valkyries. She is offering him a drink from a horn, before taking him to the feast in Odin's hall.

STONE SHIPS

Only rich and important Vikings were buried in their ships. The others were buried in ordinary graves. However, their graves were often marked out with stones in the shape of a ship. This is thought to symbolize death as a voyage into the unknown. The photograph above shows a grave in Denmark. It is one of about 200 at Lindholm Hoje in Jutland.

CREMATION

Not all Vikings were buried. Some were cremated. The Arab Ibn Fadlan described the cremation of a Viking chieftain on the banks of the river Volga in 922. First wood was piled up on the riverbank. Then the chieftain's ship was lifted on top of the pile. His body was dressed in a special outfit, which included a silk brocade coat and hat. It was carried on board and laid on a blanket and cushions inside a tent.

Food and drink for the dead man included two horses, two cows, a hen and a cockerel. A slave girl was sacrificed on board. Then the chieftain's nearest kinsman appeared, naked and carrying a blazing torch. He walked backwards to the ship and set fire to the wood underneath it. The rest of the men men came forward and threw burning torches onto the ship. When everything had burned, the ashes were placed in a memorial mound.

29

WHO·RULED·THE·VIKINGS?

The early Vikings had no rulers. The local government, called a Thing, set the laws and settled disputes. All freemen in the area had the right to vote in it. However, eventually one man in an area would become more powerful than the others. He then became their leader, or *jarl*. Some *jarls* called themselves kings, but they ruled only a small area. Later kings ruled whole countries, in Denmark, Norway and Sweden, and Things became less powerful.

THINGVELLIR

Iceland never had a king throughout the Viking Age. Instead, the people were governed by two levels of Things. The lower level of councils dealt with local matters. The other level was the Althing. This met at Thingvellir, photographed below. Thingvellir means something like legislative arena. The Althing met for two weeks at midsummer every year, because it was easier for people to travel at that time. Only the men could vote, but they took their families with them. Everyone wore their best clothes and the merchants set up booths and traded goods there. At the Althing a man called the Lawspeaker stood on a rock and recited the laws that governed the people. Juries of twelve men tried to settle disputes that could not be settled by the local Things.

Most Vikings obeyed the laws of the Things. Anyone who did not became an outlaw or *nithing*. If this happened, the outlaw had to give up all his belongings and land and had to leave the country as quickly as possible. This was because anyone could kill an outlaw without being punished. Some people were outlawed for life, and others for a number of years. Eirik the Red was outlawed from Norway in 980 and went to Iceland. Soon he was outlawed there too, but returned to tell people about Greenland.

Coins of Viking kings

THE KING OF NORWAY

The picture above is from a book called the *Flateyjarbok*. It shows Harald Finehair, the first king to rule over all Norway. He did this by defeating his enemies at the battle of Hafrsfjord in around 890.

THE JELLING STONE

The stone on the right was set up at Jelling in Denmark in the tenth century. It has three sides. The one you can see here shows an imaginary animal with a snake wrapped round its body. The second side shows a Crucifixion, and the third has an inscription. This tells us that the stone was put up by King Harald (or Harald Bluetooth) in memory of his parents, King Gorm and Queen Thyri. He became a Christian around 960 and persuaded the rest of the Danes to do the same.

· W E R E ·
THERE · ANY
VIKING
ARTISTS ?

From the evidence that has been found, it seems that there were no Viking artists who painted pictures. However, there were many Vikings who carved pictures and patterns into stone and wood. Some pictures tell stories of the Viking gods, while many of the patterns are done in what is called the "gripping beast" design. This is full of swirling lines, but when you look at them closely, you can see that there are many animals, each gripping on to the next one. Other Vikings were skilled metalworkers who worked in gold and silver.

THE OSEBERG CARVINGS

Archaeologists discovered many wood carvings on the Oseberg ship. These included four posts with animal heads, like the one on the right. The posts are carved differently, but each one had a fierce, snarling expression on its face. This was probably intended to scare evil spirits away from the area. Other carved objects found on the Oseberg ship include sledges, a wagon and a bed. Some carvings on the wagon show scenes from the story of Sigurd the dragon-slayer. Because wood soon rots, only a small amount of carving from Viking times has survived. From what has been found, however, it seems that farmers often passed their time carving patterns, probably when the weather was too bad to do anything else.

Gripping-beast brooch

METALWORK

The axe on the far left was probably made for ceremonial purposes and not meant for everyday use. It is made of iron, but a pattern has been cut into it and then inlaid with silver wire. Next to it is an early example of a gripping beast from a Swedish silver-gilt brooch. The brooch was made around 940 and the beast's paws grip its sides. Soon the designs became so complex that it is hard to decide what the beasts are supposed to be.

WOOD CARVING

These carved panels are on the wall of the church at Urnes in Norway. They were carved in the eleventh century and represent Yggdrasil, or the World Tree. This was part of Viking mythology and was thought to hold the universe together, as its branches reached the sky and covered the earth. At its base was the Well of Fate, guarded by three women called Norns who decided what would happen to all living creatures. A serpent gnawed its roots, while four deer ate the leaves and the bark, so the tree would eventually die.

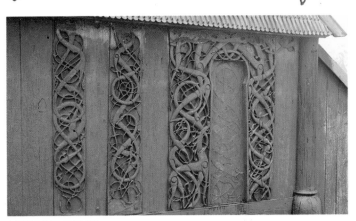

JEWELERY

The Vikings wore jewelery for practical reasons. The brooch on the left was probably used to fasten a woman's shawl or cloak. Rich people had had jewelery made of gold or silver. To make the gold sparkle really brightly, tiny chips were cut into the design to reflect the light. Poorer people wore mass-produced brooches made from cheaper metals. To make them look like gold or silver, these brooches were sometimes covered in a layer of gilt or tin.

The Middleton cross

STONE CARVING

The Vikings were skilled carvers, but they rarely carved pictures of people. This means that the cross in the drawing on the right is quite unusual. It was found at Middleton-on-the-Wolds in Yorkshire and shows a Viking warrior from the tenth century. He wears a cone-shaped helmet and has his weapons with him. These are a sword, an axe, a knife in a scabbard and a spear. Above him, the top of the cross has a pattern of interlaced lines. Other stones show scenes from Viking mythology.

DID · THE VIKINGS · WRITE · BOOKS ?

PICTURE STONES

The Vikings enjoyed telling stories about the adventures of the gods. Sometimes they carved scenes from these stories onto memorial stones. The one on the right is from a story about Odin. However, stories about Thor were most popular. The Vikings liked him best because he was not as bright as Odin. He kept getting himself into fights with the Frost Giants (see page 26) and was often in danger of being defeated. On one occasion he stole a cauldron of beer from the giants so that the gods could have a party!

RUNES

The Vikings only had sixteen letters. These letters were called runes and at first they were thought to be magic. For example, the early Vikings thought that scratching runes onto a sword would make it stronger. Later they used runes for inscriptions on memorial stones. There were not enough runes for there to be one for every sound in the language, so spelling was a difficult task for the rune carver. Translating them is also difficult. The runes are often known as *futhark* after the first six letters.

There were several reasons why the Vikings did not write any books. One reason was that they did not have an alphabet like ours. Instead they used runes which were straight, stick-like letters that could be carved on stone, metal or wood. Another reason was that they did not have any paper and did not seem to use parchment. If they wrote anything down at all, it took a long time and so they never tried anything as long as a book. In spite of this, however, the Vikings were great story-tellers and poets. They learned their stories and poems by heart and passed them on from one generation to another. Many survived and were eventually written down.

POETRY

The Vikings were very fond of poetry. When they had feasts, a poet, or *skald*, was usually invited to entertain them after the meal. He would make up new poems or recite old ones. In the poems there were a lot of *kennings*. These were a way of describing something without saying exactly what it was. For example, a sword might be called a battle-adder. Some poets traveled round the country making up verses, called *drapa*, in praise of their hosts. If the host liked the verses, he rewarded the poet with a generous gift, such as the silver armlet shown here. The most famous Viking poet was Egil Skallagrimsson. He once saved his life with a poem praising his enemy.

GOOD ADVICE

One of the Viking books, the *Havamal*, was supposed to contain Odin's advice to the Vikings, which included the following words of caution:

"Look carefully round doorways before you go in – you never know when an enemy might be there."

"Praise no day until evening, no wife until buried, no sword until tested, no ice until crossed, no ale until drunk."

"There is no better load a man can carry than much common sense – no worse a load than too much drink."

THE SAGAS

The Viking legends, or Sagas, were written down in the thirteenth century by an Icelander called Snorri Sturluson. Many of them were adventures of Vikings who had moved from Norway to Iceland. Others were histories of the Viking kings. Some books have little pictures in the margins. Those above show Olaf Tryggvason killing a wild boar and a sea ogress.

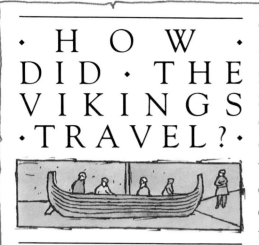

· H O W · D I D · T H E · V I K I N G S · T R A V E L ?·

The geography of the Viking homelands meant that traveling by land was very difficult. A mixture of marshes, forests, lakes and steep mountains made it impossible to travel easily for more than a few miles overland. Luckily most Vikings lived near the sea and so did most of their traveling by ship or boat. Their ships were designed to sail in shallow water as well as on the open sea. This meant that they could go a long way inland on rivers, and they could also run the ship onto a beach so they did not need deep harbors.

BUILDING A LONGSHIP

First the timber was cut and seasoned. The trunk of a tall, straight oak tree was chosen for the keel. This was laid on wooden stocks and the two curved stems were fastened to it with iron nails. Wedge-shaped planks were nailed to it, overlapping each other. Wooden ribs were fixed inside, followed by cross-beams. Then the keelson was fitted to support the mast and its sail.

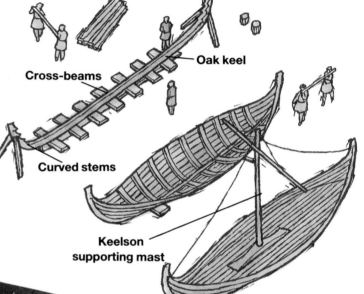

Cross-beams

Oak keel

Curved stems

Keelson supporting mast

THE OSEBERG SHIP

This ship was used for the burial at Oseberg in Norway. Earth had been piled over it. This had kept the air out and so the timbers had not rotted. Archaeologists were able to restore it so that it now looks very much as it did when it was buried in around 850. By that time the Oseberg ship was already about fifty years old. From its design, archaeologists think that it was used mainly on rivers, rather than on the sea.

THE OSEBERG WAGON

This wagon was also found on the Oseberg ship. Because it belonged to a royal lady, its wooden body was richly carved with scenes from the legend of Sigurd the Dragon-slayer. Like most Viking wagons, it was designed so that its body could be lifted off the wheels. In southern Scandinavia these decorated bodies were sometimes used as coffins for wealthy women. Everyday wagons were plainer.

SHIP CARVINGS

More evidence for Viking ships comes from the carved stones from Gotland. This one shows a ship in full sail. The Vikings could also row their ships.

Viking coins

SHIPS ON COINS

Most of the evidence for sails and rigging has long since vanished. However, some of it can be guessed at by studying pictures on coins like those drawn on the left.

NAVIGATION

Whenever possible, the Vikings sailed within sight of land. However, on the open sea they had to find their way by watching the sun and the stars. On their ships they had weathervanes with long streamers that blew in the direction of the wind. They passed directions on to each other, but even so they were sometimes blown off course.

HOW · FAR DID · THE VIKINGS · SAIL ? ·

The Vikings were great adventurers. Unlike most people in Europe at that time, they dared to sail out of sight of land. At first their journeys took them to the Faeroes, Shetlands and Orkneys. Others reached the coasts of Scotland, England, Wales and Ireland and later settled there. Swedish Vikings traveled down the rivers through Russia to reach the Black Sea and Istanbul, which they called Miklagard. Vikings from Norway started settling in Iceland in 874. From there they sailed on to reach Greenland around 980.

TRADE

The grave-goods buried with merchants in market towns such as Birka tell archaeologists a lot about how far the Viking traders traveled. For example, these drawings are based on pots probably brought back to Sweden from eastern Europe.

SETTLEMENT

More evidence for how far the Vikings traveled can be seen in Viking artefacts found abroad. This is especially true in places where the Vikings settled. At L'Anse-aux-Meadows in Newfoundland there was enough evidence to make the reconstruction of the longhouse in the photograph below.

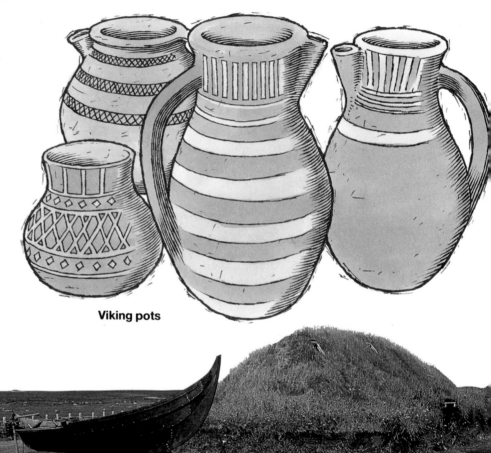

Viking pots

GREENLAND

This picture shows the remains of a Viking settlement in Greenland. Eirik the Red persuaded people to go there with him around 985. Twenty-five ships left Iceland, but only fourteen completed the journey. The settlers took animals with them and caught plenty of fish in the sea. They had to import timber, iron and grain. However, the climate worsened and eventually the farms were abandoned.

TRADE ROUTES

By sailing along rivers, the Vikings could reach the markets of Arabia. As the Arabs also traded with the Chinese, the Vikings could get goods from all over the known world.

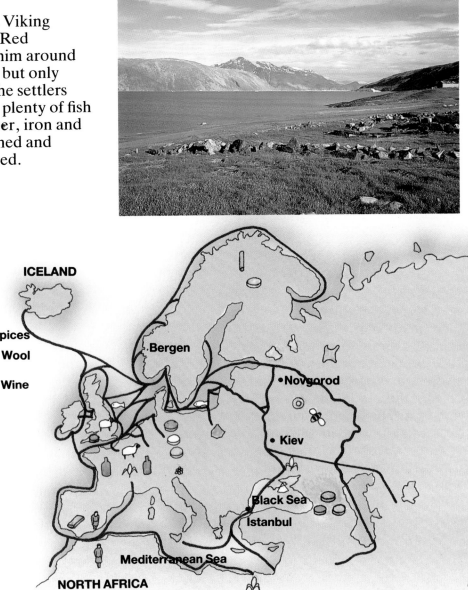

Timber   Amber   Copper   Spices

Iron   Fish   Tin   Wool

Furs   Corn   Lead   Wine

Honey   Salt   Slaves

Wax   Silver   Silks

ICELAND

Bergen

Novgorod

Kiev

Black Sea

Istanbul

Mediterranean Sea

NORTH AFRICA

SILVER HOARDS

The silver objects below are part of a Viking hoard from Cuerdale in Lancashire. A chest contained around 4000 coins. Many were Anglo-Saxon, but some were from Arabia and the continent of Europe.

TRAVEL PROBLEMS

Viking traders were always in danger of being robbed. At sea their ships might be wrecked in a storm. Even on rivers there were problems. The main one was caused by rapids, especially on the river Dnieper. To get past them, the Vikings lifted their ships out of the water and put them on wooden rollers. They could then be pushed overland and relaunched on the other side of the rapids.

DID · THE VIKINGS HAVE · AN · ARMY? ·

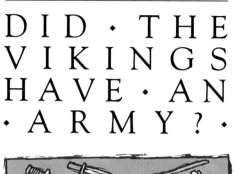

The first Vikings armies were not like armies today. They were small groups of fierce fighting men who relied on surprise to defeat their enemies. Usually they fought for themselves and not for their country. Despite their small numbers, they could frighten the kings of other countries into giving them money, called Danegeld, to go away. Later Vikings started to fight for their king, rather than for themselves. These armies were more organized. In 1016 the King of Denmark's army defeated the English at Ashingdon, and England had a Danish king.

VIKING WARRIORS

The Viking warriors did not wear a uniform. They protected their bodies with a shield and their heads with a helmet. Usually this was made of leather and fitted close to the skull like a cap. Other helmets were made of iron, rather like the one on the right. They were sometimes decorated, but never had horns or wings attached. Unlike the Lewis chessman shown below, who looks ready to fight on horseback, the Vikings usually rode to the battlefield, then dismounted and fought on foot.

Sword

Battle-axe

Shield

Spear

WEAPONS

A Viking's favorite weapon was his sword. It was used to slash at the enemy rather than stab him. They also used the battle-axe. Spears were thrown at the start of a battle and gathered up afterwards. The shield was made of wood and covered with leather. Its central boss and its rim were of iron.

BATTLE TACTICS

The Vikings armies were never very big. Because of this they had to take their enemy by surprise in order to win. If the enemy seemed likely to overwhelm them, the Vikings fought together from behind a wall of shields.

Scabbard

DANISH BARRACKS

The picture on the right is a reconstruction, based on evidence found at Trelleborg in Denmark. This site may have been soldiers' barracks. It dates from the late tenth century.

·WHAT· HAPPENED TO·THE ·VIKINGS?·

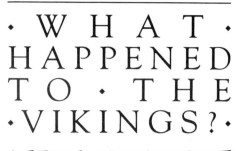

By 1100 the Viking Age was over. In places like Britain and Normandy the Vikings had settled down and married local women. In Scandinavia more land was cultivated and so young men no longer went abroad to find farms of their own. In Europe the kings had better organized armies and were able to defeat the Vikings. As populations increased, trade also changed. Merchants became more interested in goods such as grain and wool and so even the Viking traders lost their importance.

WARFARE

The early Viking attacks were successful when towns were often undefended. However, in the eleventh century European kings started building castles to defend their towns. At first the castles were built of wood, but later they were replaced by stone, like this one at Rochester in Kent. The only way to defeat a castle was by siege warfare. Vikings were unable to fight this way.

THE VIKING INFLUENCE

Although the Viking Age had ended by 1100, stone carvers in England were still influenced by Viking art. This influence can be seen today in many churches and churchyard crosses. These

Church door carvings

pillars by the door of the church at Kilpeck in Herefordshire were carved in the late twelfth century, but the carver used gripping beasts and serpents in his design, just as the Vikings would have done.

THE NORMANS

This scene is taken from the Bayeux Tapestry. This is a long strip of embroidery which tells the story of the Norman Conquest of England in 1066. William, Duke of Normandy, who became King of England in that year was descended from Rollo, the Viking who had been given the Duchy of Normandy by the King of France in 911. But the Normans had long forgotten their Viking ways. They spoke French and were all Christians. Their soldiers wore coats of chain mail.

THE VIKING HERITAGE

The Vikings gave many words to the English language that we still use today. These include everyday words such as sky, bread, egg, scrawny, snort and lump. They also gave us words such as "fell" for a hill, "beck" for a stream, "dale" for a valley and "tarn" for a pond, all of which are still used in northern England where the Viking influence was strongest. Many place-names in Britain also have their origins in the Viking Age. Those ending in "wick" were markets, those ending in "by" were villages and those ending in "haven" were harbors. Other Viking words in place-names include "ness," which means a headland, and "toft" which means a building or farm.

· GLOSSARY ·

AMBER The fossilized resin of pine trees. It is brownish-yellow in color and used for making jewelery, such as bead necklaces.

ARCHAEOLOGY The scientific study of the remains of the past.

ARTEFACTS Objects made by people.

BESIEGE To surround a place with an army so that no one can get in or out.

BROCADE A stiff silk with a raised pattern woven into it.

BYRE A building where cows are kept.

DANEGELD Money paid to the Vikings so that they would go away and not attack.

DANELAW The part of England in which King Alfred allowed the Vikings to settle. It included East Anglia and the towns of Derby, Leicester, Lincoln, Nottingham and Stamford.

DRAPA Verses made up in praise of the person who had invited the poet to his house.

FEUD A dispute between two families. It was always violent and usually involved murder.

FLAX A plant that is also known as *Linum*. The fibers of its stem are spun into yarn to make linen.

HARROW A frame of wood or iron with spikes used to push the soil over freshly sown seeds.

JET A hard black rock, related to coal.

JOLABLOT The Vikings' midwinter festival. Our word Yule is taken from this.

KEEL The part of the ship that goes from end to end and supports the whole ship.

KEELSON Part of the ship supporting the mast.

KENNING A poetic way of describing something without saying exactly what it is.

LAWSPEAKER The man who spoke the laws at the Althing. He sometimes also gave his judgement on serious matters.

MYTHOLOGY A collection of legends, usually about ancient gods.

PARCHMENT The skin of a sheep or goat that has been specially prepared for writing on.

RAPIDS A part of the river where the current is very fast and strong, usually between big rocks.

RECONSTRUCTION An object that has been made to look like the original.

RIGGING The ropes that held up the sail on a ship and allowed it to be moved.

SAGAS Stories of Viking kings and heroes (many of whom went to Iceland).

SIGRBLOT The first of the big Viking feasts each year. It took place in the early summer.

SKALD The Viking word for a poet.

THING The local meeting that governed Viking affairs.

TREATY An agreement between two people or countries.

TURF Soil that contains the roots of the grass which had grown in it.

VALHALLA Odin's hall where Vikings hoped to go when they died.

VALKYRIE One of Odin's servants who looked after the dead Vikings.

VETRARBLOT The second of the Viking feasts each year. This was celebrated in early autumn.

WHETSTONE A special stone for sharpening knife-blades.

· I N D E X ·